CREEPY CREATURES

STAR-NOSED MOLES

BY ABBY DOTY

WWW.APEXEDITIONS.COM

Copyright © 2025 by Apex Editions, Mendota Heights, MN 55120. All rights reserved. No part of this book may be reproduced or utilized in any form or by any means without written permission from the publisher.

Apex is distributed by North Star Editions:
sales@northstareditions.com | 888-417-0195

Produced for Apex by Red Line Editorial.

Photographs ©: Shutterstock Images, cover, 1, 4–5, 6, 16–17, 18, 20–21; Dan MacNeal/iNaturalist, 7, 13; Stan Tekiela/Moment/Getty Images, 9, 12, 14–15, 19, 29; E. R. Degginger/Science Source, 10–11; Skip Moody/Science Source, 22–23; Flickr, 24–25; Kirk Hewlett/Alamy, 26

Library of Congress Control Number: 2024944888

ISBN
979-8-89250-323-5 (hardcover)
979-8-89250-361-7 (paperback)
979-8-89250-435-5 (ebook pdf)
979-8-89250-399-0 (hosted ebook)

Printed in the United States of America
Mankato, MN
012025

NOTE TO PARENTS AND EDUCATORS

Apex books are designed to build literacy skills in striving readers. Exciting, high-interest content attracts and holds readers' attention. The text is carefully leveled to allow students to achieve success quickly. Additional features, such as bolded glossary words for difficult terms, help build comprehension.

TABLE OF CONTENTS

CHAPTER 1
FINDING FOOD 4

CHAPTER 2
MINI MAMMALS 10

CHAPTER 3
WATER HUNTERS 16

CHAPTER 4
LIFE CYCLE 22

COMPREHENSION QUESTIONS • 28
GLOSSARY • 30
TO LEARN MORE • 31
ABOUT THE AUTHOR • 31
INDEX • 32

CHAPTER 1

Finding Food

A star-nosed mole plunges into a **shallow** pond. The mole swims toward the bottom. Its wide feet paddle through the water.

Star-nosed moles have long tails. The moles use their tails to steer when swimming.

The mole taps its nose along the muddy ground. Its **tentacles** feel a worm in the dirt. The mole gulps down this prey.

Star-nosed moles can stay underwater for about 10 seconds. Then they must come up for air.

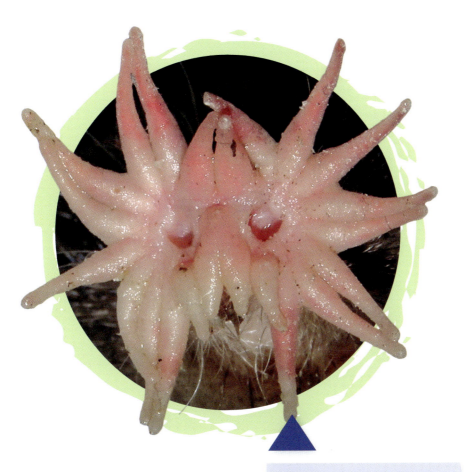

A star-nosed mole's nose has 22 tentacles.

FAST FOOD

Star-nosed moles eat faster than any other **mammal**. The moles eat too quickly for human eyes to follow. They also eat about half of their body weight in food each day.

After eating, the mole swims back to shore. It crawls into a tunnel. The mole's nose brushes against the dirt walls. It feels its way to a nest. There, the mole curls up and goes to sleep.

FAST FACT
Star-nosed moles spend about half of each day sleeping.

Whiskers on a mole's head and front feet help with its sense of touch.

CHAPTER 2

MINI MAMMALS

Star-nosed moles are small mammals. Most are about 7 inches (18 cm) long. They weigh about 2 ounces (57 g). They have short, dark fur.

A star-nosed mole's fur covers up its tiny eyes.

A star-nosed mole's tentacles move quickly. They can touch up to 12 objects per second.

A star-nosed mole cannot see well. It uses its nose instead. It feels around with its tentacles. The tentacles send signals to the mole's brain. Then, the brain makes a **mental** map of the area.

NOSE NERVES

A star-nosed mole's nose is only about 0.4 inches (1 cm) wide. But the nose holds 25,000 tiny touch **organs**. Each organ has several **nerve** endings.

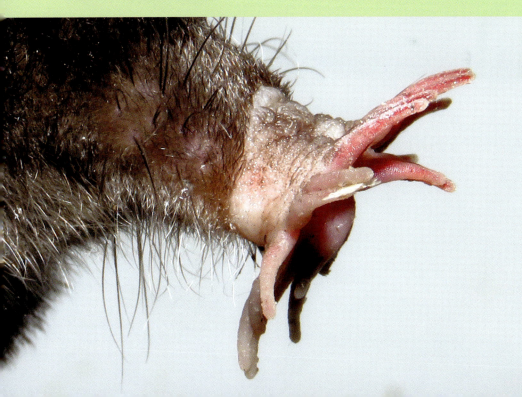

A star-nosed mole's nose has five times more nerves than a human hand.

Star-nosed moles use tunnels to nest, travel, and hunt. Their large claws can move lots of dirt. The moles can dig through 8 feet (2.4 m) of soil in an hour.

FAST FACT
Some tunnels have underwater openings. Moles swim out to hunt.

Star-nosed moles make shallow tunnels for traveling. Deeper tunnels hold nests.

CHAPTER 3

WATER HUNTERS

Star-nosed moles live in northeastern parts of North America. They make their homes in wet areas. The moles usually live near lakes, streams, or **swamps**.

Star-nosed moles are the only kind of mole that lives in swamps and marshes.

Star-nosed moles mainly eat worms and insects. The moles track prey with their noses. Their tentacles feel movements from other animals.

Star-nosed moles mostly eat underwater animals, such as leeches.

A star-nosed mole uses its bottom two tentacles to feel things up close.

UNDERWATER TRACKERS

Star-nosed moles can track animals underwater. The moles blow out air bubbles. Then they suck the bubbles back in. Smells from prey get in the bubbles. Then, the moles can follow the trail.

Usually, star-nosed moles stay safe underground. Sometimes, they search for food above ground. But many animals hunt the moles there.

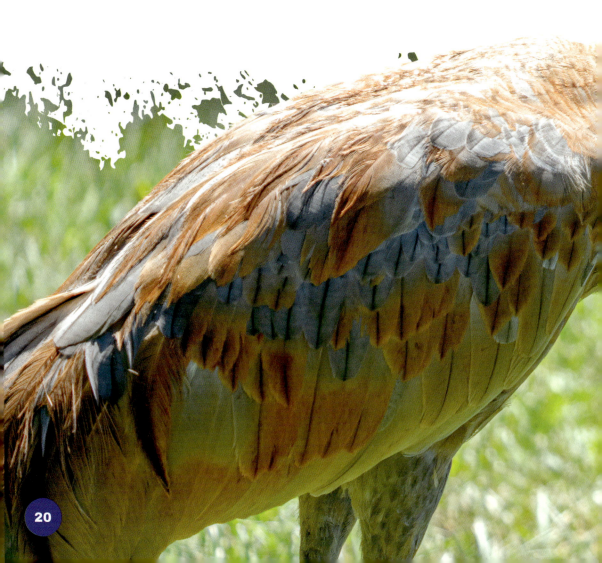

Large birds such as cranes hunt star-nosed moles.

FAST FACT

Star-nosed moles can run up to 5 miles per hour (8 km/h) when scared.

CHAPTER 4

LIFE CYCLE

Some star-nosed moles live in small groups. Others only come together to have babies. A female mole usually has one **litter** each year.

During winter, some star-nosed moles live together in tunnels.

Star-nosed mole pups are about 2 inches (5 cm) long.

Females give birth to about five pups. The pups cannot see or hear. Their eyes open after about two weeks.

MOLE PUPS

When star-nosed moles are born, their tentacles are folded against their **snouts**. The tentacles unfurl after about two weeks. That's when moles begin using them to feel.

At first, pups live together in a nest. Their mother feeds them milk. After about four weeks, the pups leave the nest. They are fully grown by 10 months old.

FAST FACT
Star-nosed moles make their nests from dry leaves and grass.

Scientists think star-nosed moles live for three to four years in the wild.

COMPREHENSION QUESTIONS

Write your answers on a separate piece of paper.

1. Write a few sentences describing how star-nosed moles hunt.

2. What fact about star-nosed moles do you find most interesting? Why?

3. How much soil can a star-nosed mole dig through in an hour?
   - A. 7 inches (18 cm)
   - B. 8 feet (2.4 m)
   - C. 5 miles (8 km)

4. Why is being underground safer for moles?
   - A. No animals hunt moles above the ground.
   - B. Many animals hunt moles above the ground.
   - C. Moles cannot find food underground.

5. What does **plunges** mean in this book?

A star-nosed mole plunges into a shallow pond. The mole swims toward the bottom.

   A. dives
   B. floats
   C. leaves

6. What does **unfurl** mean in this book?

When star-nosed moles are born, their tentacles are folded against their snouts. The tentacles unfurl after about two weeks.

   A. close
   B. spread out
   C. freeze

Answer key on page 32.

GLOSSARY

litter
A group of baby animals that are born at the same time.

mammal
An animal that has hair and produces milk for its young.

mental
Relating to the mind.

nerve
A long, thin fiber that carries information between the brain and other parts of the body.

organs
Parts of the body that do certain jobs. Organs include the heart, lungs, and kidneys.

shallow
Not deep.

snouts
The noses and mouths of animals.

swamps
Areas of low land covered in water, often with many plants.

tentacles
Thin, flexible body parts.

TO LEARN MORE

BOOKS

Rosenberg, Pam. *Gross Stuff Underground*. Mankato, MN: The Child's World, 2021.

Terp, Gail. *Star-Nosed Moles*. Mankato, MN: Black Rabbit Books, 2023.

Wilson, Libby. *Mind-Boggling Mammals*. Mendota Heights, MN: Apex Editions, 2024.

ONLINE RESOURCES

Visit **www.apexeditions.com** to find links and resources related to this title.

ABOUT THE AUTHOR

Abby Doty is a writer, editor, and booklover from Minnesota.

C
claws, 14

D
dirt, 6, 8, 14

F
fur, 10

G
groups, 22

L
litter, 22

M
mammals, 7, 10

N
nerves, 13
nests, 8, 14, 27
North America, 16
nose, 6, 8, 12–13, 18

P
prey, 6, 18–19
pups, 24–25, 27

S
sleep, 8
swim, 4, 8, 14

T
tentacles, 6, 12, 18, 25
tunnels, 8, 14

ANSWER KEY:
1. Answers will vary; 2. Answers will vary; 3. B; 4. B; 5. A; 6. B